Contents

Who was Rembrandt?

Rembrandt van Rijn was one of the greatest artists of all time. He left hundreds of paintings and drawings, signed with just his first name. Many of these are **masterpieces** of art.

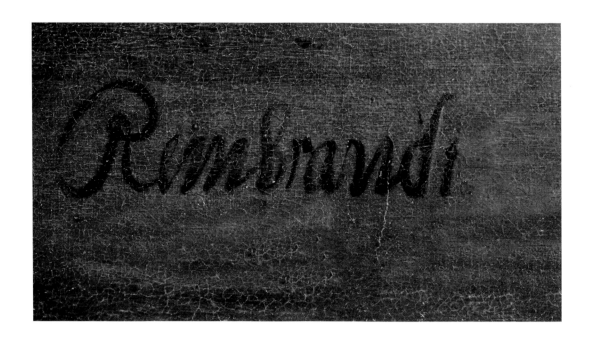

Rembrandt did over one hundred **self-portraits**. They give us many clues to his life and times. He painted this picture of himself when he was 34 and already a famous artist.

Self-Portrait, 1640

Early life

Rembrandt was born 400 years ago, on 15 July 1606, in Leiden in Holland. He had eight brothers and sisters. His father was a **miller**. He worked in one of the windmills shown on this map of Leiden.

Rembrandt did many **portraits** of his parents. He made this **etching** of his mother when he was 25, the year after his father died.

Rembrandt's Mother with a Black Shawl, 1631

Learning to be an artist

When he was 15, Rembrandt began to study art. First he studied near his home and then in **Amsterdam**. One of his teachers was Pieter Lastman, who painted this picture.

This is the first work by Rembrandt that we know of. He painted it when he was 19. It is a scene from the Bible. Look behind the kneeling figure and you will see Rembrandt's face.

The Stoning of St Stephen, 1625

Early works

In 1625, Rembrandt returned to Leiden and opened his own **studio**. He became a teacher himself. This is a drawing of Rembrandt's studio by one of his pupils. It was a very busy place.

Rembrandt painted more Bible scenes. He became good at showing light and shadow in his pictures. In this oil painting it looks as if a bright light is shining on baby Jesus.

Presentation of Jesus in the Temple, 1631

Ordinary people

In Rembrandt's time, most artists only painted important people. Rembrandt liked to walk in the town. He **sketched** old people, workers and even **beggars** he saw there.

Simeon in the Temple, 1666–69

Rembrandt used some of these drawings of ordinary people as **models** for his Bible scenes. The face of this old man is someone Rembrandt had sketched in the street.

A famous portrait painter

When Rembrandt was 25, he moved to **Amsterdam**. It was a rich and important city. There were many wealthy people living there who wanted paintings of themselves and their families.

Rembrandt was soon given his first **commission**. Nicolaes Ruts, a rich **merchant**, paid Rembrandt to paint this **portrait** of him. Rembrandt's work was very popular. In the next few years he painted nearly 50 portraits.

Nicolaes Ruts, 1631

Marriage and success

In 1634, Rembrandt married Saskia van Uylenburgh. She was a rich young woman. Later they moved to this grand house. Rembrandt filled it with his collection of paintings and works of art.

Saskia van Uylenburgh, 1634

Rembrandt and Saskia were very happy. Rembrandt painted his wife many times, in many different **costumes**. In this picture, she is wearing rich clothes and jewels.

17

Rembrandt's children

Rembrandt and Saskia's happiness did not last long. Their first child only lived for two months. Their next two children also died when they were just babies.

In 1641 they had a son called Titus. When Titus was 14, Rembrandt painted him sitting at his desk. In one hand he holds a pen and in the other his pen and ink cases.

Titus at his Desk, 1655

The artist alone

In 1642, when Titus was just a baby, Saskia became ill and died. She was only 30 years old. Rembrandt was left alone with his nine-month-old son.

The Night Watch, 1642

In the same year, Rembrandt finished his most famous picture, *The Night Watch*. It shows the town guard getting ready to go to work. Rembrandt brought the scene to life with his painting full of movement, light and shadow.

21

Landscapes

Rembrandt stopped painting so many of the
portraits which had made him rich and famous.
He spent hours walking alone in the countryside.
He sometimes made **sketches** of the places he saw.

Rembrandt drew this winter scene using pen and ink. He created a cold **landscape** with just a few strokes of his pen. He left much of the paper bare.

Winter Landscape with Cottages among Trees, about 1650

A new life

When Rembrandt was around 40 years old, he fell in love with his young servant, Hendrickje Stoffels. They later had a child called Cornelia. Rembrandt often **sketched** the family life around him.

Rembrandt's new happiness led to some of his greatest paintings. Hendrickje was the **model** for this woman bathing in a stream.

Woman Bathing in a Stream, 1654

Troubled times

Rembrandt was spending more and more money. Soon he could not pay his bills. In 1658 he had to sell his house and all his belongings. In the next ten years, Hendrickje and Titus both died.

Rembrandt never stopped painting. He finished this **self-portrait** when he was nearly 60. He is holding his **palette** and brushes and wearing his working clothes. He seems to be telling us that, in spite of all he has lost, he is still an artist.

Self-Portrait, about 1665

Rembrandt dies

Rembrandt died on 4 October 1669, aged 63. He was buried in the same church as Hendrickje and Titus. Today, Rembrandt's paintings can be seen in **galleries** all over the world.

This family **portrait** is one of Rembrandt's last paintings. He never finished it. No one knows who these people were. Was Rembrandt thinking about the family he had lost?

Family Portrait, 1668–69

Timeline

1606	Rembrandt van Rijn is born in Leiden, Holland, on 15 July.
1620	Rembrandt attends Leiden University.
1624	He moves to **Amsterdam** to study with the famous artist Pieter Lastman.
1625	Rembrandt returns to Leiden and sets up his own **studio**.
1631	He makes his home in Amsterdam.
1634	He marries Saskia van Uylenburgh.
1639	Rembrandt and Saskia buy a new home, Number 4, Breestraat.
1641	Their son, Titus, is born.
1642	Saskia dies.
1647	Around this time Rembrandt and his servant Hendrickje Stoffels live together as a married couple. She is 20 years younger than Rembrandt.
1652–4	War between England and Holland.
1654	Rembrandt and Hendrickje have a daughter, Cornelia.
1657	Rembrandt's belongings begin to be sold.
1658	His house is sold because he cannot pay his bills.
1663	Hendrickje dies.
1666	The Great Fire of London.
1668	Rembrandt's only son, Titus, dies.
1669	Rembrandt dies on 4 October, aged 63.

Glossary

Amsterdam   capital city of Holland

beggar   a poor person who asks for money

commission   being asked to make a piece of art

costume   clothes that are borrowed for dressing-up

etching   when a picture is scratched on to a metal plate

gallery   room or building where works of art are shown

landscape   picture of the countryside

masterpiece   great work of art

merchant   someone who buys and sells goods to foreign countries

miller   someone who works at a mill

model   person who poses for an artist to draw or paint

palette   flat piece of wood on which an artist mixes paint

portrait   picture of a person

self-portrait   picture an artist makes of himself or herself

sketch   unfinished or rough drawing or painting

studio   special room or building where an artist works

More books to read

Rembrandt, Life of a Portrait Painter, Great Artists, David Spence, Ticktock

More paintings to see

Rembrandt Collection, National Gallery, London

Self-Portrait, Rembrandt, National Gallery of Scotland, Edinburgh

Self-Portrait, Rembrandt, Walker Art Gallery, Liverpool

Websites

www.artchive.com/rembrandt/ rembrandt.html – shows 7 of Rembrandt's greatest paintings.

www.rembrandthuis.nl/flash. html – Rembrandt's house in Amsterdam, now a museum.

31

Index